WEEKLY WR READER®
EARLY LEARNING LIBRARY

STATES OF MATTER
Gases

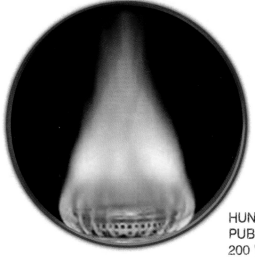

by Jim Mezzanotte

Reading consultant: Susan Nations, M.Ed., author/literacy coach/
consultant in literacy development
Science and curriculum consultant: Debra Voege, M.A., science
and math curriculum resource teacher

Please visit our web site at: www.garethstevens.com
**For a free color catalog describing Weekly Reader® Early Learning Library's list
of high-quality books, call 1-877-445-5824 (USA) or 1-800-387-3178 (Canada).
Weekly Reader® Early Learning Library's fax: (414) 336-0164.**

Library of Congress Cataloging-in-Publication Data

Mezzanotte, Jim.
  Gases / by Jim Mezzanotte.
    p. cm. — (States of matter)
  Includes bibliographical references and index.
  ISBN-10: 0-8368-6797-1 – ISBN-13: 978-0-8368-6797-8 (lib. bdg.)
  ISBN-10: 0-8368-6802-1 – ISBN-13: 978-0-8368-6802-9 (softcover)
  1. Gases—Juvenile literature. 2. Matter—Properties—Juvenile literature.
  I. Title. II. Series.
  QC161.2.M49   2007
  530.4'3—dc22   2006012965

This edition first published in 2007 by
Weekly Reader® Early Learning Library
A Member of the WRC Media Family of Companies
330 West Olive Street, Suite 100
Milwaukee, WI 53212 USA

Copyright © 2007 by Weekly Reader® Early Learning Library

Editor: Gini Holland
Art direction: Tammy West
Cover design and page layout: Charlie Dahl
Picture research: Diane Laska-Swanke

Picture credits: Cover, title, © Royalty-Free/CORBIS; pp. 5, 8, 11, 18 Melissa Valuch/© Weekly
Reader Early Learning Library; p. 6 © Adam Jones/Visuals Unlimited; pp. 9, 21 © Spencer
Grant/PhotoEdit; p. 12 © Bill Aron/PhotoEdit; p. 13 © Deb Yeske/Visuals Unlimited; p. 14
© Theowulf Maehl/Zefa/CORBIS; p. 15 © David Wrobel/Visuals Unlimited; p. 16 © Jeff
Greenberg/PhotoEdit; p. 19 © Dave Spier/Visuals Unlimited; p. 20 © Cleo Photography/PhotoEdit

Printed in the United States of America

1 2 3 4 5 6 7 8 9 10 09 08 07 06

Table of Contents

Cover and title page: Many stoves use gas flames to cook food.

Chapter One

Gases All Around

Gases are a form of matter. Do you know what matter is? It is all around you. It is anything that takes up space and has weight. Mountains and oceans are matter. So is the air we breathe. Plants and animals are matter. People are, too. Almost everything in the universe is matter.

Matter can be in different forms, or states. It can be a **solid** or a **liquid**. It can also be a gas. You can see solids and liquids. You cannot see most gases.

Matter is made up of many tiny pieces. They are called **molecules**. In solids and liquids, they stay together. In gases, they do not. Instead, they fly around. They even hit each other.

How can you hold a gas? You must keep it in a **container**. A gas always **expands**, or spreads out, to fill the container it is in. It will leak out if there is an opening. Gas spreads in all directions.

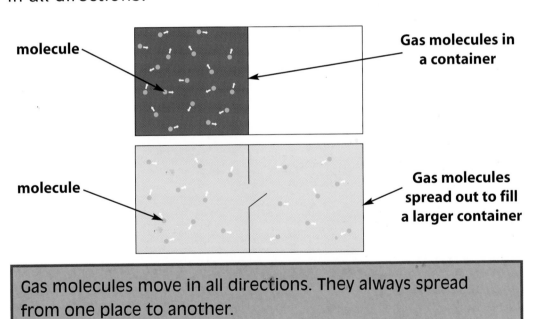

molecule

Gas molecules in a container

molecule

Gas molecules spread out to fill a larger container

Gas molecules move in all directions. They always spread from one place to another.

Gases are all around. Did you ever feel a breeze? It is the air moving. Air is different gases mixed together. We need air to survive. Gases help us in many ways!

On a windy day, you can see plants bend in the wind. This shows that air is moving. Air is made up of gases.

Chapter Two

Properties of Gases

There are many different gases. How can we describe them? The ways we describe them are called **properties**.

All gases have weight. Weight is one property of gas.

Air is a gas. Air has weight. How can we weigh the air?

TRY THIS: Find a soccer ball. Let the air out and weigh it. Then, fill it with air and weigh it again. The ball now weighs more. It has more air. The air has weight.

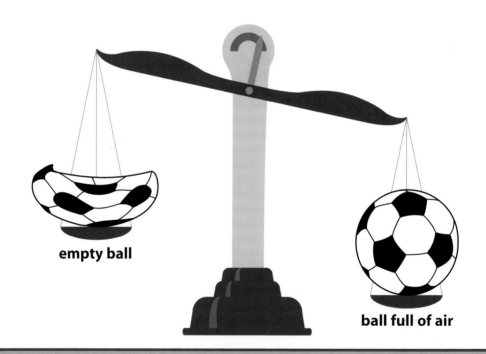

empty ball

ball full of air

The empty ball has less air than the full ball, so it weighs less.

A gas can have **volume**. Volume is the space it fills. You can measure volume. A small container has less volume. A large one has more.

What happens inside the container? Molecules bounce around. The bouncing creates **pressure**. Pressure is the gas pushing to get out.

When you blow up a balloon, you give it more air pressure.

Chapter Three

Changing and Mixing

What if you kept filling a soccer ball with air? After a while, the ball cannot get bigger. So, its volume cannot change. How does more air fit inside?

You are **compressing** the air. You put more molecules in the same space. They bounce around more often. So, there is more pressure.

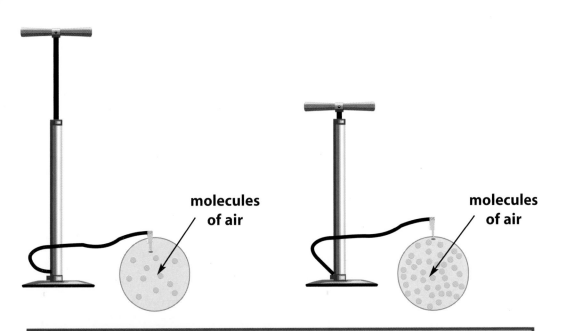

molecules of air

molecules of air

The ball on the right has more air molecules in the same space. There is more pressure in the ball on the right than in the ball on the left.

Heat makes a gas expand. What if the gas is in a container? The container cannot get bigger. The volume does not change. Instead, the pressure changes. It increases.

In a pressure cooker, air cannot escape. As the heat rises, so does the pressure. The high pressure makes food quickly in a pressure cooker.

Heat makes liquids evaporate, or turn into gas. After a storm, rain puddles seem to disappear. The Sun warms them. They turn into gas. This gas is called water **vapor**. You cannot see it. But it is in the air.

The Sun warmed puddles on this sidewalk. After a while, they evaporated.

This grass is covered with drops of dew. Dew is water vapor that turned into liquid.

Cold makes gas **condense,** or turn to liquid. Have you ever seen dew in the morning? At night, the water vapor in the air got cooler. It turned to small drops of water. Some gases must get very cold to condense.

Gases can mix together. Air is a mixture of gases. It has oxygen. It has carbon dioxide. It has other gases, too.

A gas can also mix with a liquid. Air mixes in water. Fish take in air through gills.

Did you ever see bubbles in fizzy soda? The soda has gas mixed in it. Some of the gas does not mix. It is in the bubbles.

Soda bubbles have a gas in them. It is carbon dioxide.

Solids can mix with gases, too. Did you ever see rust on a bike or car? Rust is metal, water, and the gas oxygen.

The red areas on this car are rust. It is a gas mixed with a solid and a liquid.

Chapter Four

Gases at Work

Gases are important in many ways. Oxygen is a gas. We breathe in oxygen. We need it to live.

Carbon dioxide is a gas. We breathe out carbon dioxide. It is poisonous to us. But plants need it to live. They create more oxygen for us to breathe.

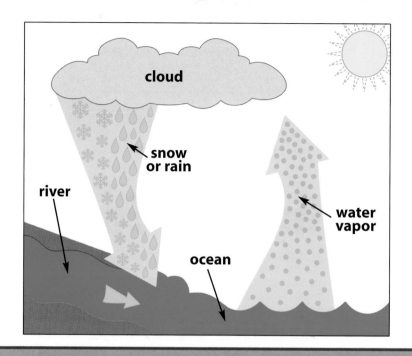

cloud

snow
or rain

river

ocean

water
vapor

Earth's water cycle never stops. During part of the cycle,
liquid water turns to water vapor.

A gas is part of the water **cycle**. All over Earth, water
evaporates. It becomes water vapor, which is a gas. The
Sun warms the vapor, and it rises. Up in the sky, it gets cool
and condenses. It forms clouds. Rain and snow fall from
the clouds.

How do you make a fire? You need oxygen. You must heat oxygen and a fuel, such as wood. They form burning gas—the flame!

When wood and oxygen get very hot, they create fire.

We can smell because of gas. A scent is really a gas. It spreads through the air to reach your nose.

We hear because of gas, too. What happens if you bang a drum? It makes air molecules move. They make other air molecules move. The moving air hits the inside of your ear.

Gas molecules from flowers move through the air. When they reach your nose, you smell the flowers!

Some gases are lighter than other gases. They have less weight. Helium is a gas. Helium is lighter than air. Helium can make a balloon float in the air.

No matter where you go, gases are at work. They are a big part of our world!

These balloons are filled with helium gas. The gas is lighter than air, so the balloons float.

Glossary

compressing — causing molecules in matter to be closer together

condense — turn from a gas to a liquid

container — something that can be used for holding other things. A container must be completely closed to hold a gas

cycle — things happening again and again, in the same order

expands — spreads out

liquid — a form of matter. A liquid cannot hold its own shape. Instead, it takes the shape of whatever holds it

molecules — tiny pieces of matter. A molecule is two or more atoms joined together. Atoms are the building blocks of all matter

pressure — the force of one thing pushing on another. A gas pushes against the inside of the container that is holding it

properties — ways of describing something. Volume and mass are two properties of a gas

solid — a form of matter. A solid can hold its own shape. This shape can be changed, but a solid will not change shape on its own

vapor — something that is in a gas form

volume — the space a gas takes up in a container, which is the amount of the gas

weight — measuring the force of gravity on an object

For More Information

Books

Gases. Elementary Physics (series). Ben Morgan. (Blackbirch Press)

Solids, Liquids, and Gases. Rookie Read-About Science (series). Ginger Garrett. (Children's Press)

Water Cycle. Nature's Patterns (series). Monica Hughes. (Heinemann)

Web Sites

Rader's Chem4Kids.com: Looking for a Gas
www.chem4kids.com/files/matter_gas.html
At this site, you can learn about gases.

Strange Matter
www.strangematterexhibit.com
Visit this site to learn about different kinds of solids.

Water
www.nyu.edu/pages/mathmol/textbook/3gradecover.html
Visit this site to learn about water as a liquid, solid, and gas.

Index

About the Author

Jim Mezzanotte has written many books for children. He lives in Milwaukee with his wife and two sons.